OXFORD
UNIVERSITY PRESS

W0051243

Oxford International Primary History

Workbook

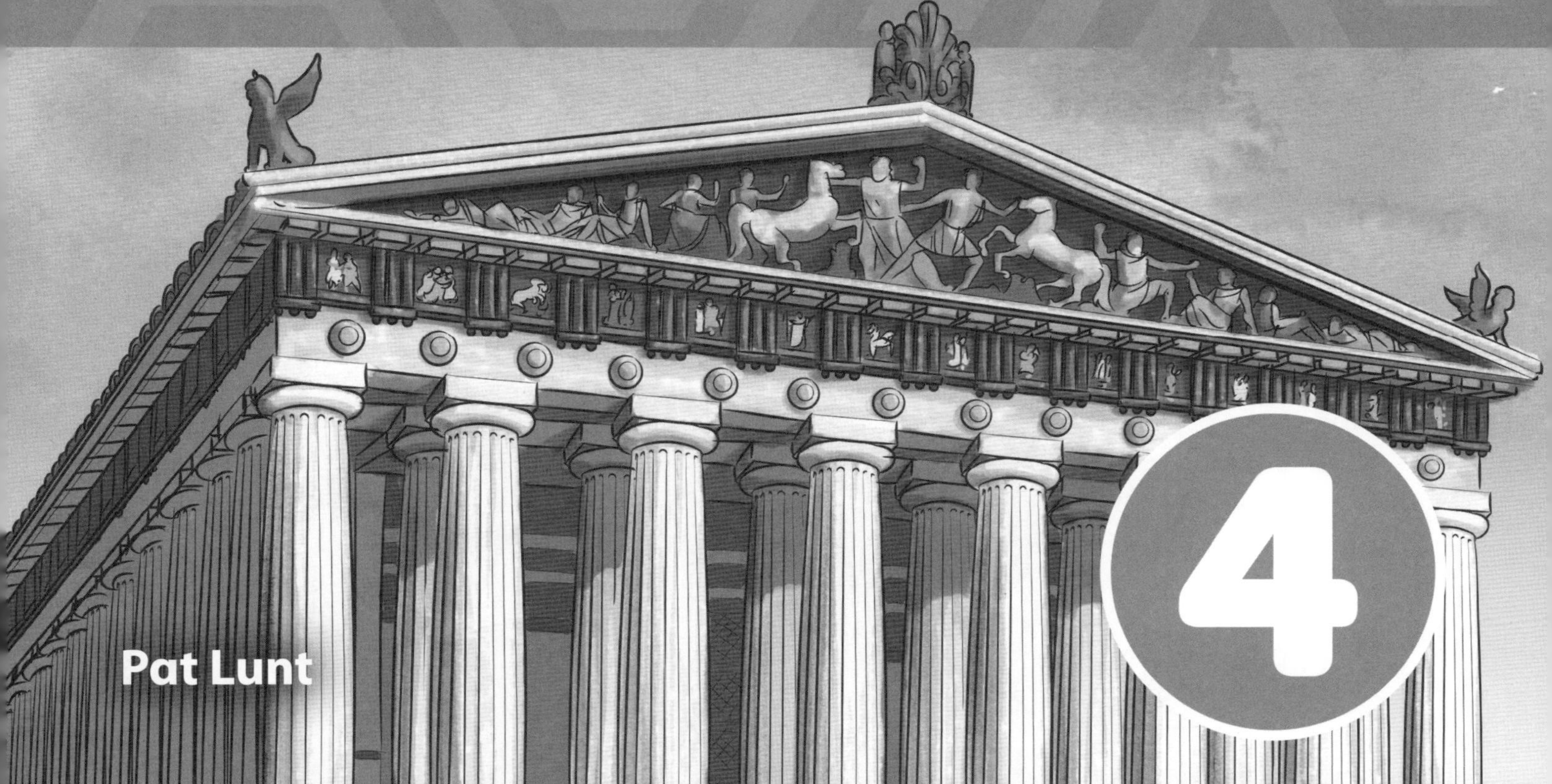

Pat Lunt

4

Oxford International Primary for enquiring minds

OXFORD

UNIVERSITY PRESS

Great Clarendon Street, Oxford, OX2 6DP, United Kingdom

Oxford University Press is a department of the University of Oxford.
It furthers the University's objective of excellence in research,
scholarship, and education by publishing worldwide. Oxford is a
registered trade mark of Oxford University Press in the UK and in
certain other countries.

British Library Cataloguing in Publication Data
Data available

ISBN: 978-0-19-841818-4

15

Paper used in the production of this book is a natural, recyclable
product made from wood grown in sustainable forests. The
manufacturing process conforms to the environmental regulations
of the country of origin.

Printed in India by Manipal Technologies Limited

Acknowledgements

Cover illustration: Carlo Molinari

Illustrations: Aptara

Photos: p19: Miroshnichenko Tetiana/Shutterstock; **p33:** Alistair
Laming/Alamy; **p39:** Sean Pavone/Alamy; **p47:** Konstantin Kalishko/
Alamy; **p60:** PSL Images/Alamy; **p61:** PRISMA ARCHIVO/Alamy;
p62: age fotostock/Alamy; **p63:** mark phillips/Alamy; **p64 (T):** Nick
Pavlakis/Shutterstock; **p64 (B):** Michael Rosskothen/Shutterstock

Although we have made every effort to trace and contact all
copyright holders before publication this has not been possible in all
cases. If notified, the publisher will rectify any errors or omissions at
the earliest opportunity.

Links to third party websites are provided by Oxford in good faith
and for information only. Oxford disclaims any responsibility for
the materials contained in any third party website referenced in
this work.

The manufacturer's authorised representative in the EU for product
safety is Oxford University Press España S.A. of El Parque Empresarial
San Fernando de Henares, Avenida de Castilla, 2 – 28830 Madrid
(www.oup.es/en or product.safety@oup.com). OUP España S.A. also
acts as importer into Spain of products made by the manufacturer.

Contents

1 Ancient Egypt

What do I already know?

What do you think are good answers to the questions in the speech bubbles? Discuss your answers with some friends. Write your answers in your notebook. Your teacher will ask you to look back at your answers when you have completed the unit.

> Where is Egypt?

> When did the Ancient Egyptian civilisation start and end?

> Why did the Ancient Egyptians build pyramids?

> What was life like for the Ancient Egyptians?

> How can we find out about the Ancient Egyptians?

Things I would like to know about Ancient Egypt

_____

_____

_____

Look at the image of pyramids on pages 4–5 of your Student Book.

1 What challenges do you think the people who built the pyramids faced?

_____

_____

2 How long do you think it took to build a pyramid?

_____

3 This is a picture of a person from Ancient Egypt called a scribe. Scribes could read and write. What do you think the scribe might be writing?

_____

_____

4 What does this image of the scribe tell us about life in Ancient Egypt?

_____

_____

_____

5 What evidence about life in Ancient Egypt did the scribes produce? How is this evidence different from the evidence we have about the Stone Age?

_____

_____

_____

1.1 Egypt and the pharaohs

Pharaohs

Use reference books and the Internet to help you make a fact file about a pharaoh.

Name	Drawing of this pharaoh
Born	
Died	
Reign began	
Reign ended	
Father	
Mother	

Two facts about this pharaoh's achievements

1

2

In 1274 BCE, the great pharaoh Rameses II fought his enemies the Hittites. Rameses ordered his scribes to write an account of the battle that took place at Kadesh. This is part of the account.

> Rameses was young and active and there was no one like him. His arms were powerful and his heart was strong. He was braver than hundreds of thousands.
>
> Every country trembled before him (Rameses). Fear was in their hearts; all the rebels bowed down for fear of the fame of his majesty.
>
> The (Hittite) chief of Kheta had come with the chiefs from many countries that were with him. Every chief brought his chariots. There were huge numbers, never seen before. They covered the mountains and the valleys; they were like swarms of grasshoppers.

Adapted from Ancient Records of Egypt, 1906

1   How does this account describe Rameses II?

_____

_____

2   How does the account describe his enemies?

_____

_____

3   Why do you think the account describes Rameses and his enemies like this?

_____

_____

1.2 Farming and trade

Farming

These pictures show the tasks involved in producing a crop of grain. The pictures are not in the correct order.

A

B

C

D

E

F

1 Write the letters in the correct order of the tasks.

_____

2 Using your correct order, write what is happening in each picture.

Step 1	Step 2	Step 3
Step 4	Step 5	Step 6

Trade

Complete this map to show the trade routes of Ancient Egypt.

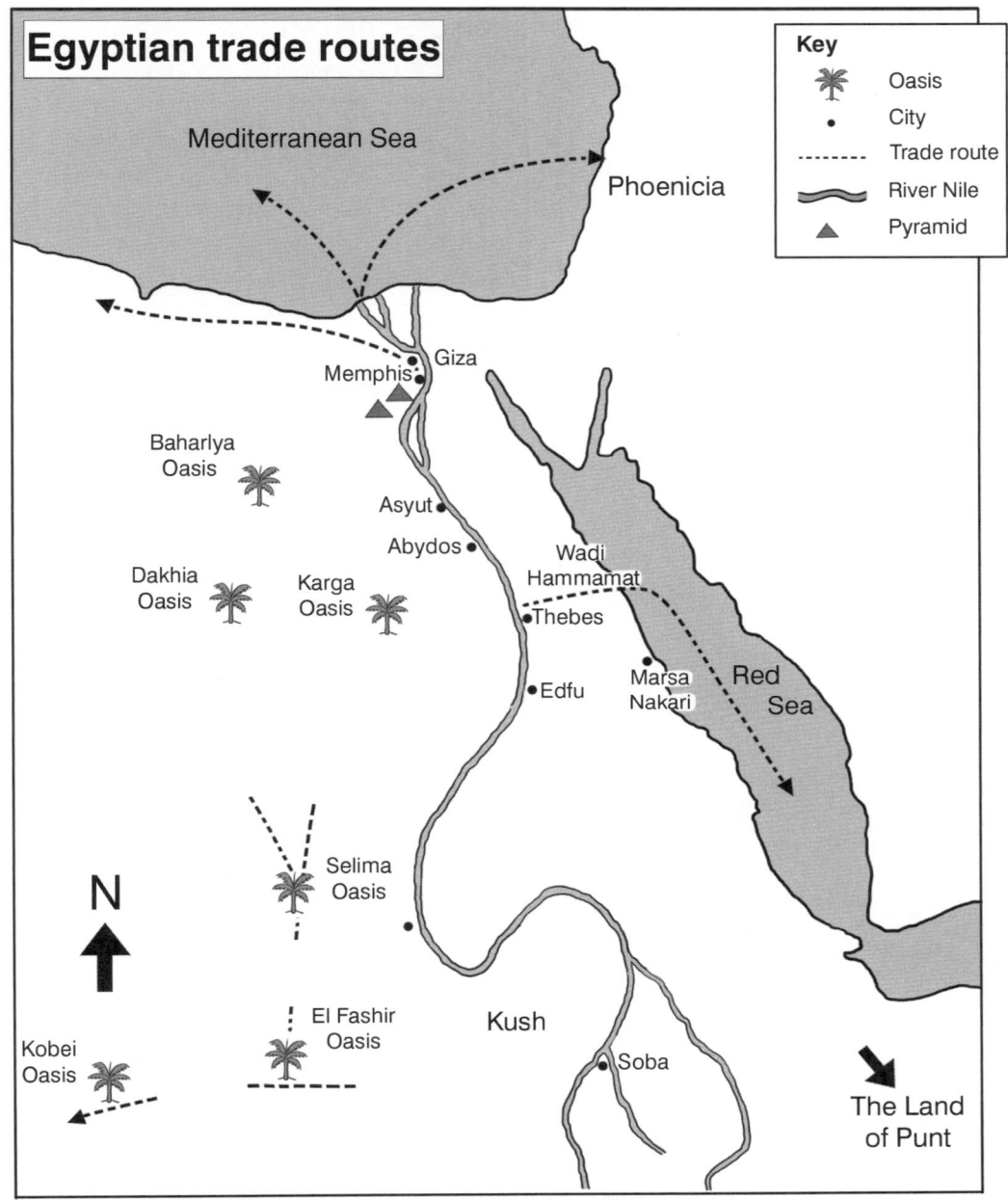

Egyptian trade routes

Mediterranean Sea

Phoenicia

Key
- ❋ Oasis
- • City
- -------- Trade route
- 〰 River Nile
- ▲ Pyramid

Giza
Memphis

Baharlya Oasis

Asyut

Abydos

Dakhia Oasis

Karga Oasis

Wadi Hammamat

Thebes

Edfu

Marsa Nakari

Red Sea

N

Selima Oasis

El Fashir Oasis

Kush

Soba

Kobei Oasis

The Land of Punt

1 Complete the trade routes between Kobei Oasis, El Fashir Oasis and Selima Oasis. Complete the trade route from El Fashir Oasis to Soba.

2 North from Selima Oasis, draw a trade route to Memphis through Dakhia Oasis and Baharlya Oasis. Draw a route to Asyut through Karga Oasis.

3 Add a trade route between Edfu on the River Nile and Marsa Nakari on the Red Sea coast.

4 Add these labels to the correct trade routes.

| To the North African coast | To Greece | To Phoenicia | To Punt |

1 Draw a line to match each item with the craftsperson who made it.

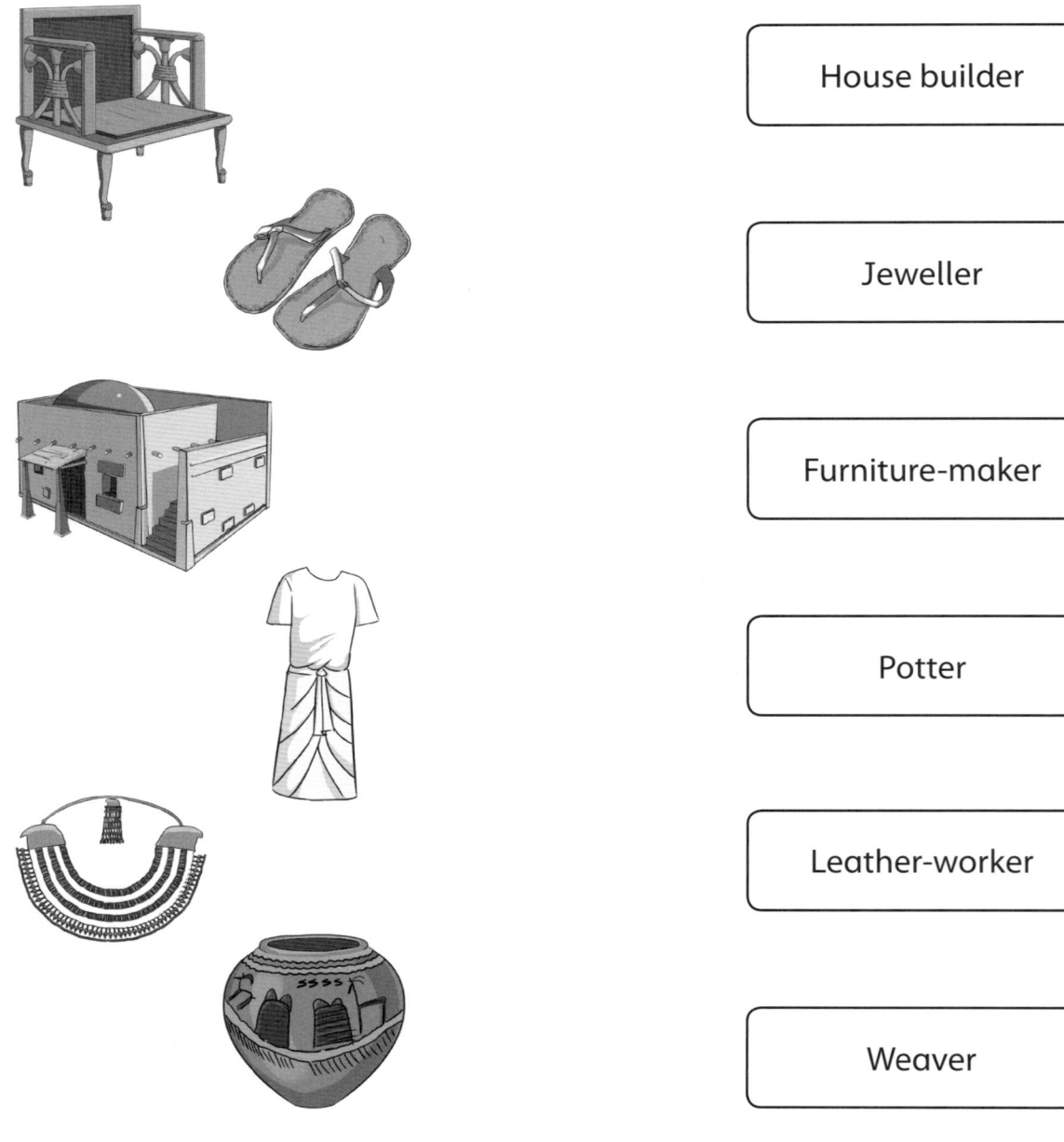

House builder

Jeweller

Furniture-maker

Potter

Leather-worker

Weaver

2 Write down two jobs from today that did not exist in Ancient Egypt. Explain why these jobs did not exist.

_____

_____

_____

House for sale

1 This is an Egyptian worker's house. Label the different parts of the house.

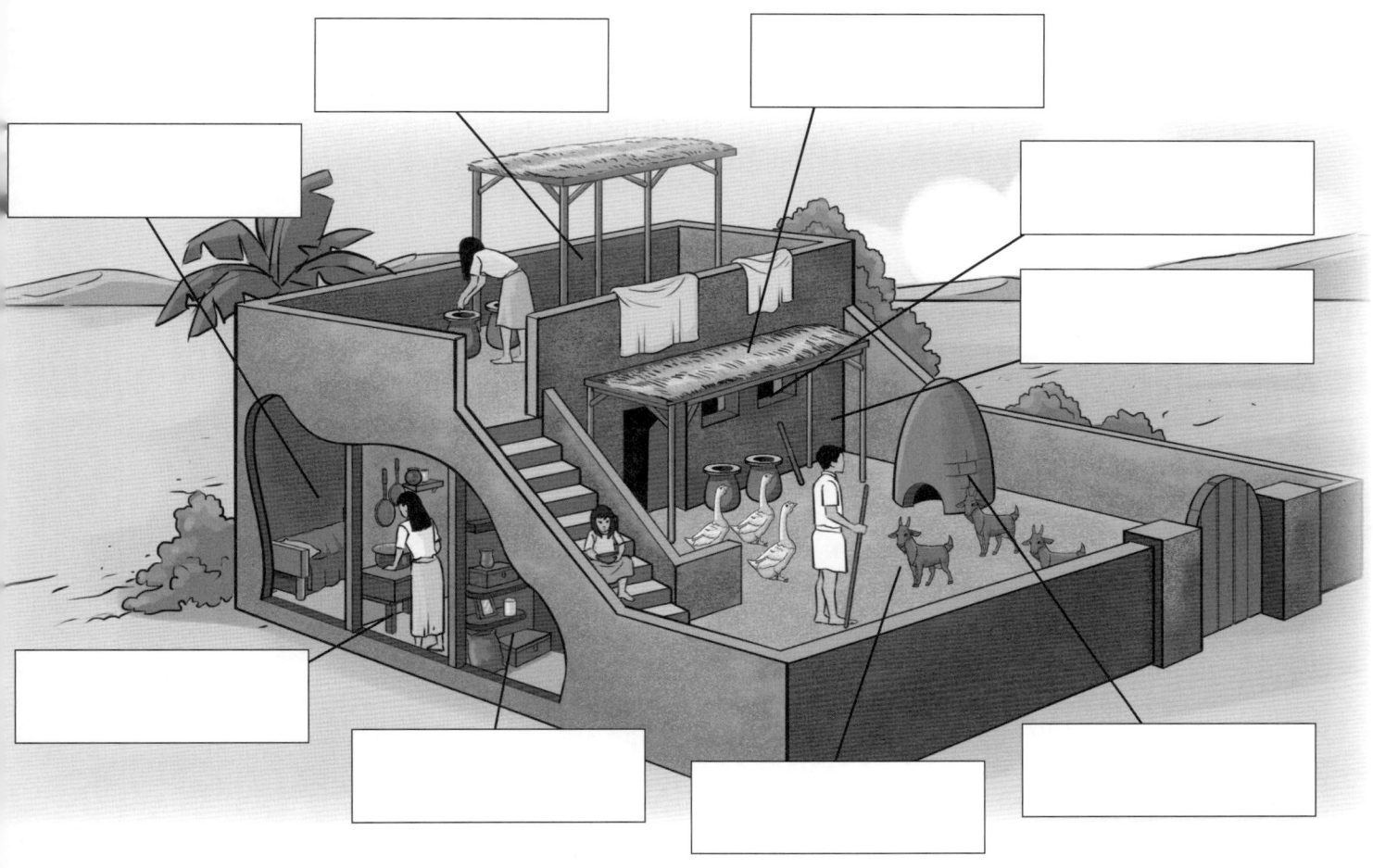

2 Write an advert for this Egyptian worker's house. Buyers will want to know how many rooms it has and how they can use each room. Include all the useful features of the house. Use the information on page 11 of your Student Book.

_____

_____

_____

_____

_____

_____

The pyramids

Here is some information about how the pyramids may have been built.

Put the steps in the correct order by numbering them 1 to 9.

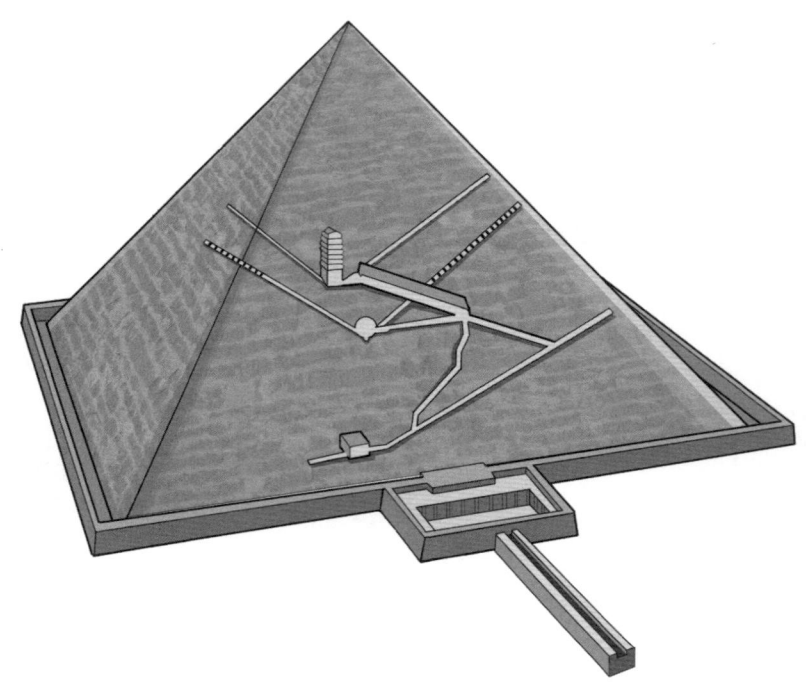

A ☐ Stone blocks are raised into position as the pyramid is built.

B ☐ The finished pyramid is covered in a layer of limestone blocks.

C ☐ Workers in quarries cut out huge blocks of stone. Some blocks weigh as much as 15 tonnes.

D ☐ The top of the pyramid is covered in a layer of gold that glints in the sun.

E ☐ Groups of workers pull the stone blocks from the river to the pyramid site.

F ☐ The site is marked so that the edges of the pyramid will face North, South, East and West.

G ☐ Stonemasons shape the blocks so that they fit together.

H ☐ Workers flatten the site for the pyramid.

I ☐ Stone blocks are transported down the River Nile to near the pyramid site.

Historical evidence for life in Ancient Egypt

Pharaohs were buried with priceless treasures and also more everyday items. Archeologists have found many objects from Ancient Egyptian tombs.

1 Write what each object tells us about everyday life in Ancient Egypt.

   a A sandal made from woven reeds

   _____

   b A wooden hippopotamus toy with a moving mouth

   _____

   c A piece of jewellery made from gold and precious stones

   _____

   d A statue of a scribe holding a reed pen and a scroll of papyrus

   _____

   e A wooden model of a sailing boat

   _____

2 Draw three of these objects here.

1.5 The Egyptian influence – evidence and inspiration

Art and writing

1 Match the words with their meanings. Use a dictionary to help you.

identical	to say what words mean in another language
hieroglyphics	people with special knowledge or skills
discovered	very old, from the distant past
experts	found during a search
translate	an Ancient Egyptian writing system
ancient	the same

2 Fill in the gaps using the words from question 1. You will need to use one of the words twice.

The Rosetta Stone dates from 179 BCE and shows writing in the Egyptian and Greek

languages. It shows three different types of writing. One is Egyptian

_____ . Another is ordinary Egyptian writing called

demotic. The other one is _____ Greek. These three types

of writing were used in Egypt when the stone was made.

The stone was _____ in 1799 by French soldiers who were

rebuilding a fort. Language _____ soon realised that the

texts were _____ . Using their knowledge of

_____ Greek they were able to

_____ the Egyptian.

Egyptian numbers and mathematics

The Ancient Egyptians were the first civilisation to use a base 10 number system – a system based on the number 10. The Ancient Egyptians used symbols to represent 1, 10, 100, 1000 and so on, but they did not have a symbol for zero.

Number	1	10	100	1000	10 000	100 000	1 000 000
Egyptian symbol							
Description	Staff	Heel	Coil of rope	Lotus flower	Pointing finger	Tadpole	Astonished man

Here are some numbers written using the Ancient Egyptian symbols.

23 = ∩∩|||

142 = ϑ∩∩∩∩||

571 = ϑϑϑ∩∩∩ ϑϑ ∩∩∩| ∩

4689 = (lotus flowers, coils of rope, heels and staffs)

Write these numbers using Egyptian symbols. The first one has been done for you.

12 = ∩||

37 =

647 =

3824 =

1 Thinking about my learning

Find your answers to the questions in speech bubbles on page 4 at the beginning of the unit. Use a different colour to add to your answers or rewrite them. Include any new information you have learned while studying this unit.

The River Nile

In some years the River Nile did not flood. In some years it flooded, but not very much. There were times when the River Nile did not flood for 50–100 years. In times without floods much less food could be produced.

1 How do you think long periods with no flooding affected the issues below? Write two sentences for each issue.

People's health
Size of the population
Trade with other countries

2 Many people think that Ancient Egypt is one of the greatest civilisations in history. Explain why you agree or disagree.

_____

_____

Thinking about my learning

☺ I understand and can do this well.

😐 I understand but I am not confident.

☹ I don't understand and find this difficult.

Learning outcome	☺	😐	☹
Explain the importance of the River Nile in Ancient Egypt.			
Analyse the structure of Ancient Egyptian society.			
Assess daily life and work in Ancient Egypt.			
Identify types of historical evidence for life in Ancient Egypt.			
Consider the influence of the Ancient Egyptians on other civilisations.			

One thing I learned about how people in Ancient Egypt lived is...

_____

_____

One difference between life in Ancient Egypt and life today is...

_____

_____

The best fact I know about Ancient Egypt is...

_____

_____

One thing I would still like to know about Ancient Egypt is...

_____

2 Ancient Greece

What do I already know?

What do you think are good answers to the questions in the speech bubbles? Discuss your answers with some friends. Write your answers in your notebook. Your teacher will ask you to look back at your answers when you have completed the unit.

Where is Greece?

When did the Ancient Greek civilisation start and end?

What was life like for the Ancient Greeks?

What did the Ancient Greeks do for fun?

How can we find out about the Ancient Greeks?

Things I would like to know about Ancient Greece

_____

_____

1 Look at the image of the carving on pages 18–19 in your Student Book.

   a What do the soldiers have to protect themselves?

   _____

   b Look at how the soldiers are arranged. What does this tell you about how the Greek army fought in battle?

   _____

   _____

   c What weapons can you see?

   _____

   d How do you think soldiers from an enemy army felt when they faced the Greek army?

   _____

   _____

2 The Ancient Greeks used large clay jars like this to store and transport food. The clay jars tell us something about life in Ancient Greece.

   a What food items do you think the Ancient Greeks stored in these jars?

   _____

   _____

   b What do people use to store these food items today?

   _____

Ancient Greek city-states

1 Write on this map the names of the Greek city-states that are shown. The first letter of each name has been given for you.

C

A

M

S

K

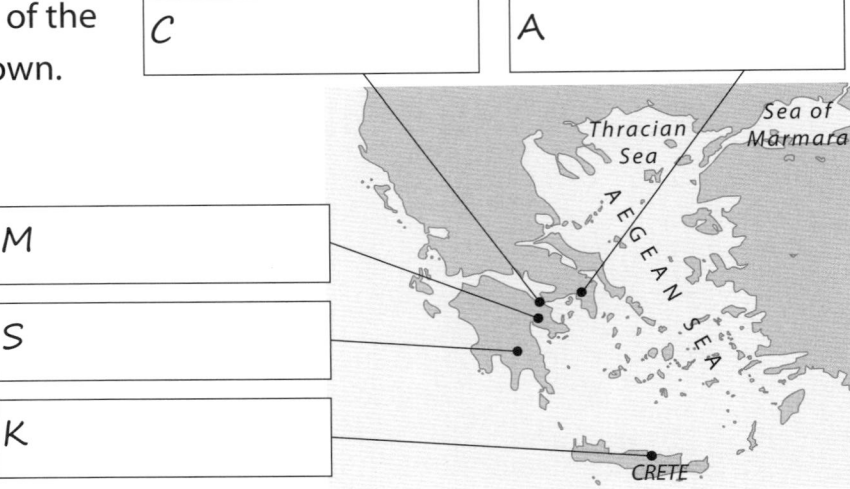

Thracian Sea

Sea of Marmara

AEGEAN SEA

CRETE

2 Fill in the fact file for one of the city-states. Use reference books and the Internet to help you.

Name of city	Name of region
Population	Drawing of an ancient coin
Surrounding landscape	
Nearest port	
Famous person	Drawing of one famous building
Important event in the city	
Interesting fact	

Ancient Greek geography

This drawing is based on a map made by Hecataeus of Miletus. Experts think the map was made in about 520 BCE. Use an atlas and other resources to answer the questions.

1 What does the map tell us about what the Ancient Greeks knew about the world?

_____

_____

2 How did the Ancient Greeks gain this knowledge about the world?

_____

_____

3 Find out the modern names of the countries, rivers and seas shown on the map.

_____

_____

4 Why is the land on the map surrounded by 'Oceanus'?

_____

2.2 Work and relaxation in Ancient Greece

Work in Ancient Greece

Describe these jobs in Ancient Greece. Do some research and use the words in the boxes to help you.

Teacher

boys	girls	reading	writing	history	mathematics

_____

_____

_____

Potter

clay	potter's wheel	household	plates	jars

_____

_____

_____

Furniture-maker

wood	oak	beech	saw	chisel	nails
glue	bed	chair	table	bench	

_____

_____

_____

Leisure in Ancient Greece

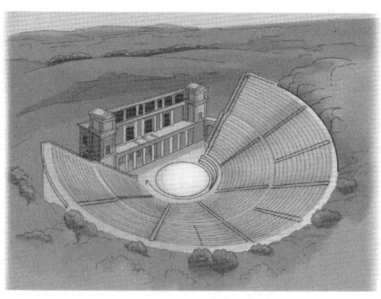

What happened in this place in Ancient Greece?

_____

Draw a modern version of this building.

What are these children doing?

_____

Where did people in Ancient Greece do this type of activity?

_____

What physical activities did people do in Ancient Greece?

_____

_____

What are these people doing?

_____

What type of building are they in?

_____

Draw people doing this activity in Ancient Greece.

2.3 Everyday life in Ancient Greece

Life at home in Ancient Greece

Answer these questions about how the Ancient Greeks got food and clothing. Use pages 24–25 of your Student Book, reference books and the Internet to help you.

1 Who was responsible for getting the food a family needed? Where did the food come from?

_____

_____

2 Where did people get their clothes? Who made sure the family had the clothes they needed?

_____

_____

3 Draw a picture of the room used by women in a Greek house. Show some of the furniture and other objects. Add labels to show how people used these objects.

The different lives of young women and girls

1 This is a small statue of two young women playing knucklebones. The statue was found in Athens. What does the statue tell you about life for young women and girls in the city-state of Athens?

_____

_____

_____

_____

2 Read this extract from the writings of Xenophon. He was a writer born in Athens in 431 BCE. In an essay called *Laws of the Lacedaemonians,* Xenophon wrote about rules made by a law-maker from Sparta called Lycurgus.

> Lycurgus believed motherhood to be the most important function of women who were not slaves. He introduced races and trials of strength for women competitors, the same as for men. He believed that if both parents were strong they would produce stronger children.

Adapted from *Laws of the Lacedaemonians*

3 Look at the statue of the girls and read the extract by Xenophon again. Explain why the statue was probably not from Sparta.

_____

_____

_____

The battle of Marathon

The 5th century Greek historian Herodotus wrote a book called *Histories*. In the book, he described a battle in 490 BCE between the Athenians (with their friends the Plataeans) and an invading Persian army.

> The two armies fought on the plain of Marathon for a long time. Part of the way through the battle the barbarians were victorious. The Persians broke the Greek lines in the centre and chased them inland. On the edges of the battlefield, the Athenians and the Plataeans defeated the Persians. They easily made the Persians run. Instead of chasing them, the Athenians joined the fighting in the centre and won. Then the Athenians chased their enemy all the way to the shore. In this battle of Marathon about 6400 Persians and about 192 Athenians died.

Adapted from *Histories,* by Herodotus

1 What does Herodotus think about the Athenian soldiers?

_____

_____

2 Herodotus was a Greek historian. Do you think his account of the battle is completely accurate? Explain why.

_____

_____

Challenge

Find out why a running race of 26 miles (42 kilometres) is called a marathon.

War at sea

How were the different parts of a Greek warship used? Complete the table.

Part of the ship	How it was used

Local history study

The Ancient Greeks made ships for war and for trade. Find out about traditional boat or ship building near where you live. What were the boats or ships used for? Did the ships or boats travel along rivers or across the sea? What were they made from? Use reference books and the Internet to find out.

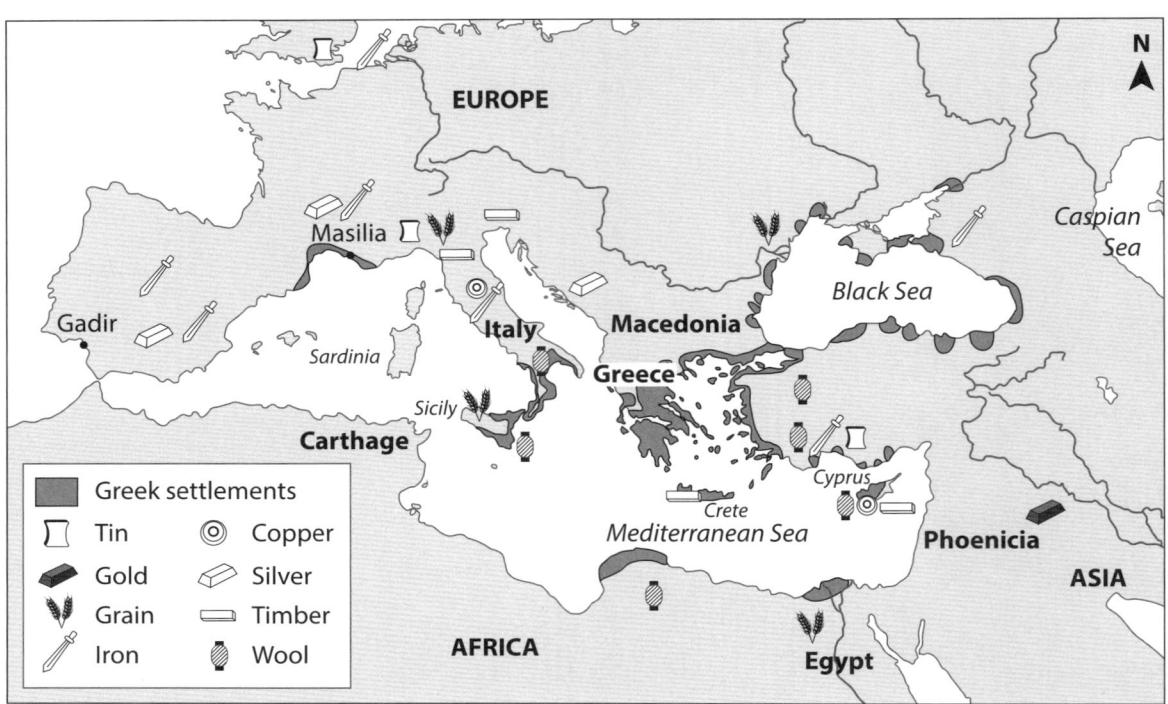

Use the map and an atlas to help you complete the table. Use modern names for countries or regions.

Resources	Imported from
Metals for tools and weapons	
For shipbuilding and house construction	
For clothes and blankets	
For bread-making and porridge	

Language

Many English words are made using Ancient Greek words. Here are examples of Ancient Greek words or parts of words and their meanings.

Greek word/part	Meaning	Greek word/part	Meaning	Greek word/part	Meaning
aero	wind, air	*anti-*	against	*bio-, -biotic*	life
eco-	environment, habitat, home	*geo-*	Earth, world	*-graph, -graphy*	write, record, describe
kilo-	one thousand	*-logy, -ology*	science	*-meter*	measure
micro-	tiny	*-phone*	sound, voice	*photo-*	light
-scope	see, sight	*tele-*	far away	*thermo-*	heat

The words below are made using parts from Greek words. Use the table above to work out the meaning of each word. Then use a dictionary to find out the definition. Then do the same for one more word made from Greek parts.

Word	Meaning of the parts	Dictionary definition
Ecology	environment + science	
Geography		
Telephone		
Thermometer		

2 Thinking about my learning

Find your answers to the questions in speech bubbles on page 18 at the beginning of the unit. Use a different colour to add to your answers or rewrite them. Include any new information you have learned while studying this unit.

Life in Ancient Greece

1 What do these pieces of historical evidence tell us about life in Ancient Greece?

a An Ancient Greek coin found in North Africa	
b A room containing tall clay jars	
c A painted plate with farming scenes	
d The sunken wreck of a trireme	
e Ruins of important buildings	
f Written histories	

2 'The Ancient Greeks influenced many civilisations throughout history and still have an influence today.' Explain why this is true.

_____

_____

_____

Thinking about my learning

☺ I understand and can do this well.

😐 I understand but I am not confident.

☹ I don't understand and find this difficult.

Learning outcome	☺	😐	☹
Explain who the Ancient Greeks were.			
Analyse and describe everyday life in Ancient Greece.			
Describe how the Greeks fought wars on land and at sea.			
Consider the influence of the Ancient Greeks on other civilisations.			

One thing I learned about how people in Ancient Greece lived is…

_____

_____.

One difference between life in Ancient Greece and life today is…

_____

_____.

The best fact I know about Ancient Greece is…

_____

_____.

One thing I would still like to know about Ancient Greece is…

_____

3 Ancient Rome

What do I already know?

What do you think are good answers to the questions in the speech bubbles? Discuss your answers with some friends. Write your answers in a notebook. Your teacher will ask you to look back at your answers when you have completed the unit.

What is an empire?

Why did the Romans make an empire?

What was life like in Ancient Rome?

How can we find out about the Ancient Romans?

Why do we remember the Ancient Romans?

Things I would like to find out about Ancient Rome

_____

_____

_____

Look at the image and answer the questions. Use your Student Book
pages 32–33 to help you.

1 Why do you think the Romans constructed this building?

_____

_____

2 Why did the Romans have one of these buildings in almost every large town
or city in their empire?

_____

_____

3 Do any modern buildings look similar to this building in some ways?

_____

_____

4 What are these modern buildings used for?

_____

_____

3.1 The beginnings of Ancient Rome

The Roman Republic

The sentences below are not in the correct order.

1 Write the numbers 1 to 7 in the boxes to show the correct order of the sentences.

A ☐ The Roman tribe rebelled in 509 BCE and removed the last Etruscan king.

B ☐ The Roman tribes were ruled by kings from the Etruscan tribe.

C ☐ The Roman Republic lasted until 27 BCE.

D ☐ Some Etruscan kings were cruel.

E ☐ Before Rome was established, the people on the Italian peninsula lived in different tribes.

F ☐ The Etruscan kings had complete control and made all the decisions.

G ☐ Rome became a republic and the Roman people elected different citizens to be their leaders.

2 Why do you think the Romans rebelled against the Etruscans?

_____

_____

3 Explain one difference in how the Romans were ruled before and after they rebelled.

_____

_____

The people of Ancient Rome

Describe what life was like for the three groups of people in Ancient Rome shown in the table. Write about:

- how much money or land they had
- the types of work they did
- how much control they had over their own lives.

Life in Ancient Rome	
Patricians 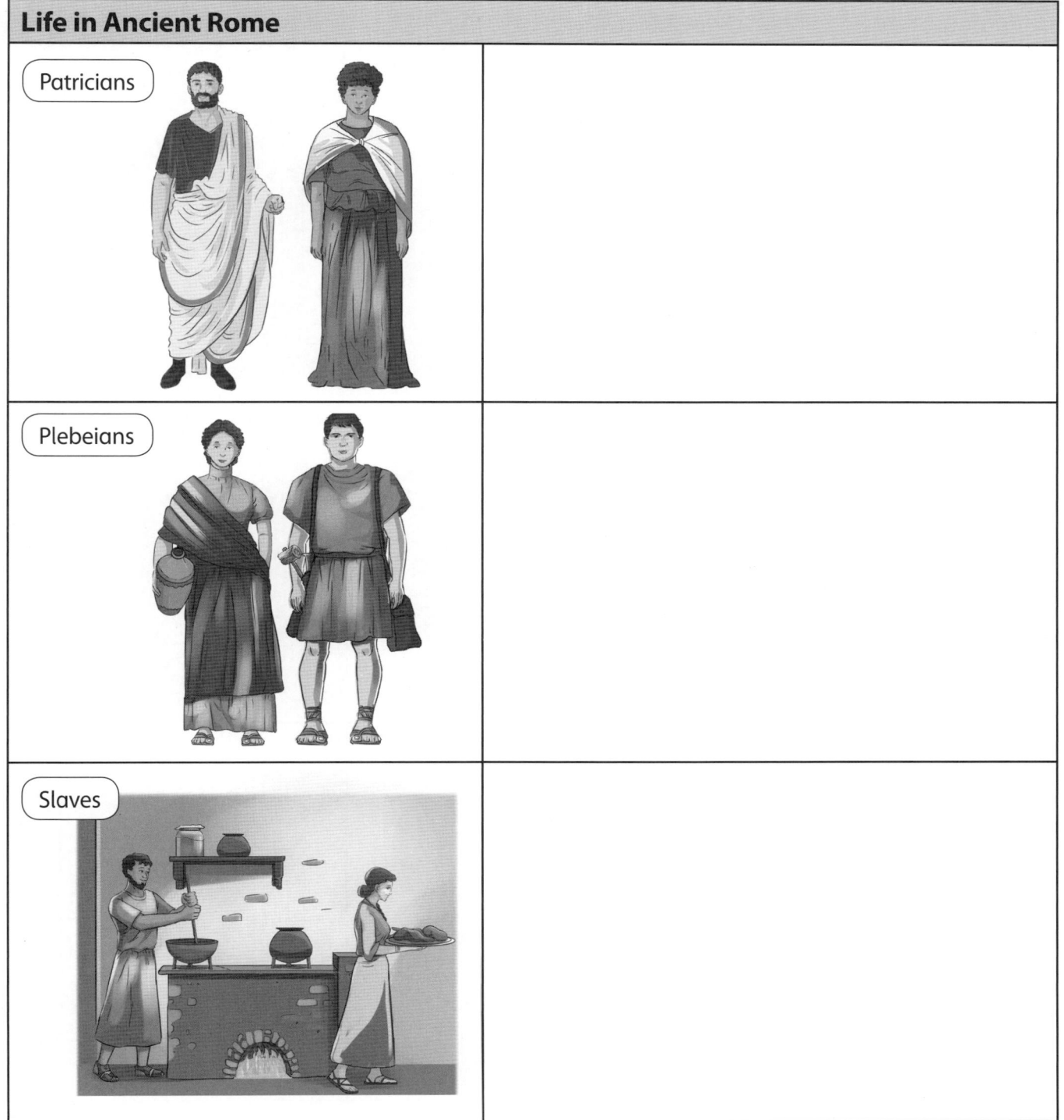	
Plebeians	
Slaves	

3.2 The Roman Empire begins

Territories of the Roman Empire

The map shows the area covered by the Roman Empire at its greatest extent.

1 Use an atlas to work out which modern countries were part of the Roman Empire.

2 Find out about Roman towns and cities in those countries. Complete the table for three towns or cities in different modern-day countries. An example has been done for you.

ATLANTIC OCEAN

Rhine

Caspian Sea

Black Sea

Danube

Tigris

Euphrates

Mediterranean Sea

Nile

Red Sea

Key

Roman Empire, 117 CE

Modern town/city name	Roman name	Modern country	Date founded or occupied by Romans	Main purpose
Merida	Emerita Augusta	Spain	25 BCE	To protect a pass and bridge on a trade route

3 Mark your three cities on the map.

Resources for the Roman Empire

Resources were traded across the whole Roman Empire. Some resources were brought into the empire. The resources allowed the Romans to do many things.

Look at the list of some of the resources that the Ancient Romans used.
Draw a line to match each resource with how the Romans used it.

Resource

Salt

Lead

Iron

Limestone

Olives

Oak timber

Uses

to make oil for cooking and cleaning

to make concrete

for construction and ship building

to make weapons and tools

to make water pipes and cooking pots

to flavour and preserve food

Local history study

1 Ask members of your family to help you research these questions.

- Are any of these resources used in your country today?

- Where do these resources come from today?

- What are these resources used for today?

2 In your notebook explain some similarities and differences between life in Roman times and life today. Use all your work on this page to help you.

In an Ancient Roman town

1 Name two things in the picture that the government of the town had to provide and look after.

_____

_____

_____

_____

2 Read these descriptions and write the name of the building or structure.

a A building with many two-roomed apartments where poorer people lived

_____

b A place for chariot racing or horse racing

_____

c A large round building where people watched gladiators fight

_____

d A semicircular building with seats in rows, very similar to buildings found in Ancient Greece

_____

e A place where people could meet and also wash

_____

Water supply in Ancient Rome

In about 75 CE, a Roman historian called Pliny the Elder wrote a book called *Natural Histories*. In one part of the book he wrote about an aqueduct built by the Emperor Claudius.

The aqueduct produced by the costly works begun by the Emperor Caligula and completed by Claudius is better than all earlier aqueducts. The waters in this aqueduct are carried a distance of 40 miles. They are carried at such a high level that even the hills on which Rome is built are supplied with water. There is plenty of water for public baths, ponds, canals, private mansions, public gardens and country estates close to the city. The achievement of supplying all this water is added to the distance the water travels before entering the city. Also impressive is the height of the arches, the tunnelling of mountains and the levelling of routes across deep valleys. When everything is looked at, this must rate as the most remarkable achievement anywhere in the world.

Based on Pliny the Elder's *Natural Histories*

1 How far was the source of the water from the city of Rome?

_____

2 What was the water used for when it reached the city?

_____

_____

3 Which parts of the aqueduct did Pliny think were particularly impressive?

_____

_____

3.4 Everyday life in the Roman Empire

Food in the Roman Empire

1 Fill in the gaps using the words from the box.

wealth	sauce	simple	evening	spices
bread	meat	porridge	vegetables	

Most people in Ancient Rome had a _____ diet. They ate fresh

_____ and fruit. They also used grain to make

_____ and _____ . People ate their largest meal

of the day in the _____ . Richer families ate more

_____ . People showed their _____ by having

more expensive food. Food was often served in a _____ and

flavoured with _____ .

2 Read through the sentences in question 1. In your notebook write what we can learn about life in Ancient Rome from the food that people ate. Use these questions to help you structure your writing.

a Where did most of the Ancient Romans' food come from?

b Which jobs were needed to get the food to Romans living in towns and cities?

c What were the differences between the food eaten by richer people and poor people's food?

d Where did the more expensive and exotic foods come from?

e What does your answer to **d** tell us about trade in Ancient Roman times?

Farming in the Roman Empire

Many people in Ancient Rome owned farms. Some farming families produced only enough food to feed themselves. Some rich people owned farms in the country. They hired people to work on the farms for them.

In about 160 BCE, a man called Cato the Censor (234–149 BCE) wrote these ideas about buying a farm.

The farm should be in a place where labour and cattle are available. There should be a good, natural supply of water. The farm should be near a good sized town. It should be either on the sea or a river that can be sailed on by ships or boats. If not, the farm should be on a good and busy road...

Adapted from Cato's writings

Complete the boxes to explain why each of these things was important for an Ancient Roman farm to be successful.

Water supply	Rivers and roads

A successful farm needs...

Labour	Cattle

3.5 Art and culture of Ancient Rome

Ancient Roman mosaics

A mosaic is a picture made from many small pieces of coloured stone or glass. The small pieces are called tesserae. Mosaics were a popular type of art in Ancient Rome. The mosaics showed patterns or images of people, animals and plants.

 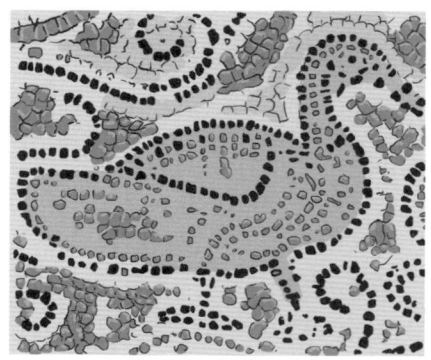

1 Use reference books and the Internet to find an example of a Roman mosaic design showing an animal or a pattern. Copy and colour the design.

2 Write some facts about the mosaic you have copied. When was it made? Where was it found? What does it show?

Eye-witness accounts

These passages are from a letter, written by a man called Pliny the Younger to the Roman historian Cornelius Tacitus. The letter describes what happened to Pliny and his uncle, Pliny the Elder, in 79 CE. Pliny the Elder was a naval commander.

It was early in the afternoon of 24th of August. My uncle had been reading his books when my mother pointed out a cloud of unusual size. My uncle called for his shoes and climbed up to higher ground. The cloud was rising from a mountain. Afterwards we learned that the mountain was Vesuvius.

Later, Pliny the Elder learned that people were in danger. Pliny the Younger wrote about the rescue boats.

Ash was falling onto the ships now, hotter and thicker the closer they went. Meanwhile on Mount Vesuvius broad sheets of fire and leaping flames blazed. Their bright glare was made clearer by the darkness of night. The ships were in danger of running aground because the sea had gone out quickly. Also huge boulders were rolling down the mountain and blocking the shore.

Adapted from *Selected Letters of Pliny*

1 What is Pliny the Younger describing?

_____

2 Discuss, in a small group, why writings such as this letter from Pliny the Younger are valuable sources of historical evidence.

Challenge

Find out about the city of Pompeii and what happened in 79 CE. Discuss, as a class, why Pompeii tells us a lot about Roman cities.

3 Thinking about my learning

Find your answers to the questions in speech bubbles on page 32 at the beginning of the unit. Use a different colour to add to your answers or rewrite them. Include any new information you have learned while studying this unit.

Pax Romana

Caesar Augustus came to power in 27 BCE. For 200 years afterwards there was a period of time known as the 'Pax Romana'. This means 'Roman Peace'. There was much less war and fighting during the Pax Romana.

1   Read this information about the Pax Romana.

	No other civilisation could challenge the Roman army. Instead of fighting, the Romans developed new technology. The Romans made road networks across their empire. They made aqueducts to supply water for drinking, washing and bathing.

Here are some effects of the Pax Romana:

- The towns and cities the Romans built were better than what was there before.
- People who lived in conquered territories could become Roman citizens. They could own land and become wealthy.
- The Romans took the best farming lands for themselves.
- Territories conquered by Rome had to pay taxes.
- People from conquered territories could be made to be slaves or even killed.

2   Think about your answers to these questions. Discuss your answers in a group.

   a   Do you think everyone thought that the Pax Romana was a good thing?

   b   What do you think were the good things about the Pax Romana?

   c   Who do you think suffered during the Pax Romana?

Thinking about my learning

☺	I understand and can do this well.
😐	I understand but I am not confident.
☹	I don't understand and find this difficult.

Learning outcome	☺	😐	☹
Explain who the Ancient Romans were.			
Compare different ways in which Ancient Rome was ruled.			
Explain why the Romans were so successful at creating an empire.			
Analyse and describe everyday life in Ancient Rome.			
Consider the influence of Ancient Rome on other civilisations.			

One thing I learned about how people in Ancient Rome lived is...

_____

_____

One difference between life in Ancient Rome and life today is...

_____

_____

The best fact I know about Ancient Rome is...

_____

_____

One thing I would still like to know about Ancient Rome is...

_____

4 A history of leisure and recreation

What do I already know?

What do you think are good answers to the questions in the speech bubbles? Discuss your answers with some friends. Write your answers in a notebook. Your teacher will ask you to look back at your answers when you have completed the unit.

What is leisure time?

What things affect the amount of leisure time a person has?

What activities do people do in their leisure time?

How has what people do for fun changed over time?

How can we find out what people did for fun in the past?

Things I would like to know about the history of leisure and recreation

_____

_____

_____

Look at the image and answer the questions.

1 What game are the boys in the photo playing?

_____

2 Who plays this game?

_____

3 What equipment is needed to play the game?

_____

4 Do you think the game is very popular?

_____

5 What other games like this do people play?

_____

6 Why do people like to play these games?

_____

Children's toys in ancient times

Find out about a simple children's toy that children from an ancient civilisation played with. Draw the toy in the box on the left. Answer the questions with facts about your chosen toy.

	Which ancient civilisation did the toy come from?
	How old is the toy?
Where was the toy found?	
What is the toy made from?	
How did children play with the toy?	

Board games at home

1 Carry out a survey to find out how many people in your family play board games and video games. Use the table to collect your results.

Name of family member	Name of board game	How often played?	Year when last played?

Name of family member	Name of video game	How often played?	Year when last played?

2 Share your results with the class. Then discuss these questions.

• Do more people play video games than board games? Why?

• Do people play video games alone or with other people?

• What are the similarities and differences between games from the past and games today?

How sports developed

Many sports developed from skills that were needed for other purposes such as hunting or war.

Look at the information in the boxes on the left. Think of a modern-day sport that is based on each of these ancient skills. On the right, draw a picture of the modern sport. Write two facts about each modern sport.

> Bows and arrows were used for hunting in the Stone Age. People in ancient civilisations also used bows and arrows as weapons in war.

> This drawing is of a carving from Ancient Greece. It shows a warship powered by oarsmen. A much more ancient carving from Azerbaijan from about 10 000 BCE shows about 20 people in a simple boat.

Local history study

Find out about a traditional sport or game in your country. In your notebook write what the sport is, when it started and why it developed.

Changes in sport over time

1 The table is for information about sports played today and sports played in the past. Choose two sports. Use pages 50–51 of your Student Book, your own knowledge and the Internet to help you complete the table. An example has been done for you.

	Sport 1	Sport 2	Sport 3
Sport played today	Lacrosse		
Is it played in a special place?	Lacrosse field		
Some countries that have a national competition	Australia, Canada, Norway, Wales		
Is there an international competition?	World Lacrosse Championships		
Does your country have a national team?			
Was the sport played in Ancient Greece or Rome?	No		
Is there an ancient version of the sport?	Mohawk Native American game of begadwe. This game dates back to the 12th century CE.		

2 Prepare ideas for a class discussion about the similarities and differences between sport today and in ancient times.

4.3 Have people always gone on holiday?

History of tourism

Local history study

Work in a group. Prepare a presentation for the class about the history of tourism where you live. Include international and domestic tourism. Domestic tourism is when people travel in their own country for pleasure. International tourism is when people travel to other countries for pleasure. Use reference books, the Internet and holiday brochures. Write notes for your presentation in the table.

Examples of early tourism where I live
Early tourist attractions: Which places did people visit?
Which tourist attractions do people visit today?
When were the first hotels built?

How has the tourism industry in your country grown in the past 50 years?
Main sea ports 50 years ago: Main sea ports today:
Main airports 50 years ago: Main airports today:
Number of tourists 50 years ago: Number of tourists today:

History as a tourist attraction

Local history study

Complete the fact file about a historic place in your country that is a tourist attraction. Draw or stick images in the boxes. Use your own knowledge and information from holiday brochures and tourist guide books.

Name of the attraction	
Location	
Type of attraction	
Age of the attraction	
Special features of interest to tourists	

Two images of the attraction

Create another fact file in your notebook for a different historic place in your country.

Theatres in history

1 Draw and write about the features of theatres throughout history.

Drawing of an Ancient Greek theatre	Three facts about Ancient Greek theatres
Drawing of a 17th-century theatre	Three facts about 17th-century theatres
Drawing of a modern theatre	Three facts about modern theatres

2 Write one way in which theatres through history have stayed the same and one way in which they have changed.

_____

_____

Film and cinema

1820 ——→ 2020

These sentences are not in the correct order. Write the letter and date for each sentence in the correct place on the timeline.

A 1895 French brothers Auguste and Louis Lumière presented the first moving picture show to a paying audience of more than one person.

B 1927 'The Jazz Singer' was the first film with spoken words.

C 1832 Belgian Joseph Plateau and sons introduced the phenakistoscope. This toy created the illusion of movement.

D 2009 The 3D film 'Avatar' became the highest-earning film of all time.

E 2017 It was the 80th anniversary of the release of 'Snow White'.

F 1906 The first animated cartoon was produced.

G 1827 The first still photo was taken.

H 1889 Thomas Edison and W. K. Dickson developed the kinetoscope. This device passed film in front of a light. Only one person could watch the film at a time.

I 1937 'Snow White' was the first full-length animated film released by Walt Disney.

J 1995 The first feature-length computer-animated film – 'Toy Story' – was released.

Local history study

Ask members of your family at home about the films they remember watching as children. Ask about their experiences of going to the cinema and of watching films at home. Talk about your findings in a class discussion about how cinemas and film technology have changed over time.

4.5 Educational recreation

The history of museums

You have been asked to create a new 'Museum of Museums'. Your museum will tell the story of the history of museums. Complete the floor plan by writing some examples of objects to display in each room. Draw a picture of one exhibit in each room.

The Museum of Museums

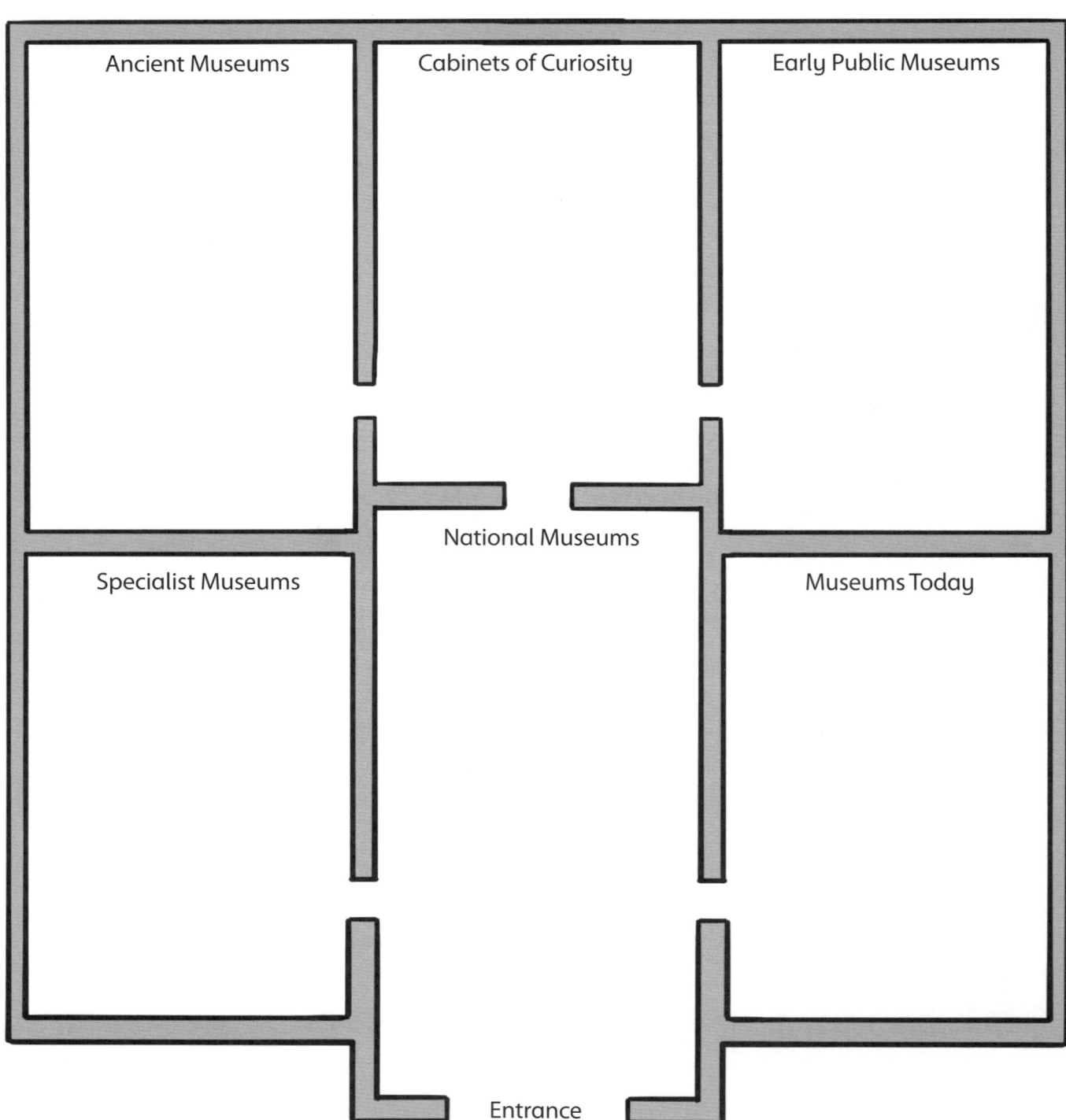

Ancient Museums

Cabinets of Curiosity

Early Public Museums

Specialist Museums

National Museums

Museums Today

Entrance

A museum for today

1 In the future, museums will show what life was like in the time we are living in now. What items will be shown in these museums?

   a Choose one theme from the following: transport, communications, clothing, food, homes, work or entertainment.

   b Choose one object from today that is a good museum exhibit for your theme.

   c Draw a picture of your exhibit in the space below.

2 Write a short label to explain what the exhibit is and why it is important. Write as if the exhibit is from the past. For example, this label is for a car:

> In the early 21st century people still drove around in personal vehicles called cars. Cars rolled on wheels over the ground instead of hovering like our vehicles today. People drove cars on special surfaces called roads.

Theme
Drawing of the exhibit
Label

2 Put all your ideas together as a class and create an exhibition in your classroom.

4 Thinking about my learning

Find your answers to the questions in speech bubbles on page 46 at the beginning of the unit. Use a different colour to add to your answers or rewrite them. Include any new information you have learned while studying this unit.

Different ways of enjoying free time

1 'People have always enjoyed playing games and sports.'
  Write three sentences, using examples of games and sports, that support this statement. For example, you could:

  A Name and describe some ancient activities that have developed into sports.

  B Name and describe a traditional sport or game from a particular country.

  C Name and describe some modern sports or games.

  D Describe how people from different groups in a society played games and sports.

  E Name and describe some toys or games played in the past.

  _____

  _____

  _____

  _____

  _____

2 Explain some changes in transport in the 19th and 20th centuries that allowed more people to take holidays.

  _____

  _____

Thinking about my learning

> 🙂 I understand and can do this well.
>
> 😐 I understand but I am not confident.
>
> 🙁 I don't understand and find this difficult.

Learning outcome	🙂	😐	🙁
Define the terms 'recreation' and 'leisure time'.			
Identify different forms of recreation over time.			
Describe ways in which recreation and leisure time have changed.			
Compare and contrast different forms of recreation over time.			

One thing I learned about the history of leisure and recreation is...

_____

_____

One difference between leisure and recreation in ancient times and today is...

_____

_____

The best fact I know about the history of leisure and recreation is...

_____

_____

One thing I would still like to know about the history of leisure and recreation is...

_____

_____

Glossary

Using your own words, explain what these words mean.

agora

architecture

atrium

board game

city-state

dynasty

Egyptologist

hieroglyphics

hoplite

museum

pyramid

republic

sarcophagus

stadium

theatre

tournament

trireme